ISBN 9781099319150

Bpeace (Business Council for Peace)

50 Hill Street #257
Southampton, New York 11968

WomenForward@bpeace.org

Mentoring Women Forward

The 2019 Playbook

Insights and action steps for any organization, woman or man to use in making their own corner of the world more inclusive, diverse and successful.

Compiled and edited by
Joan Harper and Toni Maloney

Published by the Business Council for Peace (Bpeace)

CONTENTS

PART I
Aligning Business Strategy

PART II
Changing Corporate Culture

PART III
Overcoming Obstacles Through Systemic Change

PART IV
Boosting a Woman's Power to Advocate

When a woman's potential is championed,
a whole society moves forward.

PREFACE
An Accidental Book

We serendipitously decided to publish this playbook.

In early 2019, the nonprofit organization I lead had just closed a nationwide call for nominations for the first Bpeace Women Forward Awards. Our primary goal was to shine a light on organizations and people who were successful at advancing women forward. We intended to hold the winners out as inspiration and role models for the businesses and women the Business Council for Peace (Bpeace) advises in historically violent communities like El Salvador and Guatemala. Our secondary goal was to hold a celebratory breakfast event for the winners as a fundraiser for our work.

But as we conducted video interviews with the nominees, we realized that we had tapped into a gold mine of rich detail about how these organizations and people succeed and the impact they are achieving. We saw that compiling the stories into a playbook would multiply the effect of these efforts by providing a guide for others to replicate.

If you would like to learn more about mentoring women forward or explore additional details on the programs described in this book, email us at *womenforward@bpeace.org*.

Our thanks to those who made this event and playbook possible:

The Skillanthropists (Bpeace business volunteers) who collaborated at the leadership level, including Alpa Pandya, Angela Scalpello, Dana Kuznetzkoff, Lauren Leland Brand, Maribeth Fox and Victoria Summers.

Our blue-ribbon panel of judges: Alicia Hamilton of Worth; Lisa Hetfield of the Rutgers Institute for Women's Leadership; Kathleen King, founder of Tate's Bake Shop; and Karen Vander Linde of Merryck & Co.

The champions for the nominees, including Aaron Galileo, Amanda Granath, Ann Callison, Barbara Bylenga, Beth Cowperthwaite, Bob Eng, Catherine Banat, Carole Southall, Clara Henning, Corinne Walker, Elaine Reiss, Jaime Latzman, Jane Gannaway, Jordan Less, Leslie Pesante, Liz Wald, Madeleine Wiener de Torsiac, Madison Kominski, Mark Johnson, Mathangi Srinivas, Melinda Kerins, Ruth Kreiger, Ryan Alvarez, Taylor Bolton, and Valerie Peck.

Our Women Forward Awards partners who spread the word: Plum Alley, Rutgers Institute for Women's Leadership, Women in Technology International, and Worth.

The Bpeace staff team, including Alexandra Salas, Ana Jerolamon, Florence de Sola, Joan Harper, Lauren Hass, Marcela Figueroa, Marla Gitterman, Mike Bento, Nicoletta Penzo, Sally Fay, Sam Ehsani and Stephany de Gonzalez; book designer Mirko Pohle; and our friends at Yellow Web Monkey, Pause for Thought, and Business Wire.

The Cornell Club–New York and our friends from the entertainment industry who contributed to the celebration for our winners: Amy Hargreaves, Condola Rashad, Erin Darke, Geneva Carr, Jessica Hecht and Sakina Jaffrey.

Toni Maloney
Bpeace Co-founder and CEO
May 2019

Despite the fact that women account for 47 percent of the U.S. labor force and 53 percent of the college-educated workforce, they still lag behind men and occupy only 10 percent of top management positions in S&P 1500 companies.

Unless otherwise noted, the statistics that appear here and on subsequent facing pages are taken from "Women's Leadership by the Numbers" by Judith Warner, Nora Ellmann and Diana Boesch, posted on November 20, 2018, by Center for American Progress (americanprogress.org).

Foreword
Stop Admiring the Problem
and Do Something

Angela Scalpello and Alpa Pandya are strategic advisors to C-suite executives at Fortune 500 and private equity firms, global institutions and startups. Scalpello's focus is on aligning leadership teams with growth strategies. Pandya is known for uncovering transformative insights that lead to impactful and ambitious strategies. Both also volunteer their time and expertise as "Skillanthropists" with the Business Council for Peace (Bpeace) whose mission is the economic empowerment of women in historically violent communities.

Let us reframe the problem: Struggling organizations view diversity and inclusion as one more business challenge. Successful organizations, on the other hand, accept that diversity and inclusion can be the solution to their real business challenges:

Competition. You are competing for customers, clients, users, subscribers. Are women key to your sales growth, maybe even critical to reversing a shrinking market share?

Talent. Currently, unemployment is low in the U.S., and most organizations are competing for talent. In truth, you will always be competing for the best talent. Are you making policy decisions and building a culture that will attract and retain women?

Innovation. In a world where constant innovation is essential to remaining competitive and viable, don't you want to be among the winners that unleash the full, ground-breaking potential of a diverse and inclusive workforce?

Teamwork. In today's matrixed operating environments where teamwork is the way things get done, does your culture foster and reward collaboration through focused efforts on diversity and inclusion?

Representation. Over 80 percent of purchase decisions are made by women. In addition, women are the predominant household gatekeepers and community influencers. Why sublimate this perspective when it carries so much weight in our society?

The data is clear. Studies by McKinsey and others find that companies with more diverse employees at every level grow their customer base, win top talent and make better decisions—all leading to better financial returns. **Moving women forward and having a more inclusive workforce goes beyond being the right thing to do. It's the smart business thing to do.**

Yet even as awareness has grown about the "whys" of moving women forward, many organizations are still stuck on the "how." The good news is there are many ways to approach it, and they are described in this playbook. Legacy brands, disruptive innovators, and individual women (and men) who have championed rising stars their entire careers generously share their experiences in moving women forward so that you can replicate their actions where you work.

We know that everyone can find at least one small step to take away from this book, or an array to implement in a sweeping refresh to move you closer to your business or career goals.

Only read on if you are prepared to do something. Because standing still while admiring the problem is not an option. Winning in a business world racing toward the future at warp speed will take all kinds of hands on deck. **All kinds.**

Alpa Pandya
Angela Scalpello
May 2019

There are only 33 women CEOs in the Fortune 500.

Part I
Aligning Business Strategy

Follow the growth. Need more customers, clients, subscribers? Shift the paradigm and make strategic market-facing decisions to attract women.

But as the companies here did so effectively, changing the way you appeal to women purchasers also results in creating new internal policies to drive change.

Women constitute 61 percent of accountants and auditors but are only 13 percent of chief financial officers in Fortune 500 companies.

Financial Times
Marching to a Million Readers by Tilting to Women

The decline in print advertising and a move to digital content can create an insecure and uncertain revenue stream for news media. Few media outlets have been able to offset this decline in ad revenue with subscription revenue alone. However, the Financial Times (FT) found success with its paywall model and was looking for more ways to grow. Research conducted around FT readership found that one avenue worth exploring to achieve this goal was to attract and engage more women.

To widen and diversify its audience, FT chose to review how its journalism was presented and received by more diverse readers to learn ways it could improve. At the same time it was adapting hiring, promotion and retention practices. This was a true outside-inside alignment that helped the 130+-year-old publication cross the million-subscriber threshold.

According to Kirsty Devine, FT's U.S. Head of HR and Global Projects, all the moving parts worked in sync because they were driven by the single-minded business strategy: March to a Million paid-for readers.

"This is not a focus on gender diversity and gender inclusion because it's the thing that everyone is doing nowadays," Devine says. "No, this is the

FT's business strategy, and this is a real untapped readership opportunity we're all working toward."

The FT effected change by:

• Providing clarity around its business strategy to grow its subscriber base by increasing female readership.

• Activating this strategy by giving editorial the resources required to create products with a female readership in mind.

• Changing internal HR practices around specific goals: achieving gender parity percentages in all departments; recognizing the particular needs of women returning from maternity leave; inserting women into succession-planning pipelines; engaging in innovative partnerships to elevate women's confidence and presentation skills.

* * *

In Devine's own words

"A big part of the FT's March to a Million strategy was to broaden and diversify our readership, especially among females. When we looked at our demographics, we found an untapped opportunity around females reading and engaging with FT content. We found they weren't spending as long on FT.com or commenting on articles as their male counterparts.

"Subsequently, various editorial, commercial and product initiatives were born.

"We realized we needed different voices on FT.com, so we began to feature our female journalists and columnists more predominantly, as well as creating a newsletter curated by female journalists called 'Long Story Short.'

"Our product team designed the 'She said He said' newsroom bot to analyze how many sources are male or female within FT stories. Its purpose is to demonstrate to our editors where we need more diversity in attribution.

"Opinion editor Brooke Masters is a strong advocate for increasing the number of female opinion writers. She is making sure we are tracking not just gender diversity but also ethnicity and geographical location of contributors. Last year the number of female opinion writers was 30 percent.

"JanetBot tracks the number of women featured in images on the FT home page. The tool's name pays tribute to Former Federal Reserve Chairman Janet Yellen, who was featured in no fewer than three articles on the day the bot was first prototyped.

"The FT is basing these efforts on research showing a positive correlation between stories including quotes of women, to higher rates of engagement with female readers.

"All of the data curated is being used to raise awareness to FT editors at certain times of the day when they are curating content for our pages. In essence, we are asking them use the data to inform which content will appeal most to a diverse audience.

"We started with gender, and we are now broadening into other areas and dimensions of diversity. This led us to thinking about what it feels like to be a woman working at the FT, and what we can do to help to ensure that women feel included and that they have a great positive experience here.

"For our internal alignment, our first step was to set goals for a 50-50 gender parity on our senior leadership team by 2022. We also set goals for certain departments where females were underrepresented, such as technology.

"Next we tackled HR practices and looked at family-friendly benefits. We extended our paid maternity leave globally—all staff receive 20 weeks paid maternity leave. We introduced a new flexible working approach driven by the guiding principle that we believe any role can be performed with some degree of flexibility. While there is no stringent process around this, staff are encouraged to have conversations with their manager and HR will provide as much support as needed.

"The new HR practices also include returner coaching to females returning from maternity leave; and for recruitment, we now have 50-50 male-female shortlists in place.

"Like many firms, we have global women's affinity groups. FT Women is a big part of our initiative and is empowered to provide tangible and motivating initiatives for staff.

"In the areas of training and mentoring, we launched 'Define Your Success' aimed at advancing females at different stages in their career. We also partnered with the 30% Club in the U.K. and offered mentors and mentees opportunities to learn more about female representation on executive boards and senior leadership roles.

"In the U.K., we also partnered with the Royal Central School for Speech and Drama for a confidence-building session around projecting and how women can present themselves in a room.

"Finally, as if we weren't serious enough about our general company mandate, we have a 'No Manel' policy—no FT employees can participate in external panels featuring male speakers only.

"We are on a journey, and there is a long way to go. We are excited to share and build on all that we have done and all that we have learned so far."

Taking action on the FT's experience

• Take note: Many times pursuing external growth goals to reach more diverse audiences/consumers/customers paves the way for internal changes that need to be made.

• Provide managers with real-time data to inform them of the nuances of their decision making and how this affects gender inclusiveness.

• Ground changes in HR policy to specific goals, not just "nice to have" programs.

Women are 50.8 percent of the U.S. population, but only 25 percent of the state and federal government representatives in the Senate and House of Representatives.

Anheuser-Busch InBev
Inclusivity Strengthens Consumer Demand and Employee Opportunity

Anheuser-Busch (AB) InBev is the world's leading brewer, with operations in over 100 countries, employing nearly 180,000 colleagues. The company dream is to bring people together for a better world.

The beer industry's advertising and marketing efforts as a whole have been traditionally very male dominated, even though women purchase over 75 percent of beer sold and drink over 30 percent of all beer consumed worldwide.

AB InBev first addressed this gender imbalance as an opportunity to grow its consumer base with advertising and marketing shifts. This was led by internal champions who innovated with an integrated and global effort for inclusivity at all levels of the business and across the value chain.

Today nearly half of AB InBev's U.S. breweries are led by female brewmasters, and three of the company's top brands are helmed by women.

AB InBev effected change by:

• Partnering with #SeeHer, a movement to ensure accurate portrayal of girls and women in media, which inspired the 2019 International Women's Day campaign for Budweiser, the world's most valuable beer brand. AB InBev was the first and only alcohol company to join at the advisory level.

• Launching the Women in Beer Global Mentoring Program to ensure that AB InBev women were getting the support and visibility needed to advance.

• Training AB InBev management on how to effectively sponsor women; traditionally people mentor women on soft skills and mentor men on business results.

In her own words: Jodi Harris, Vice President, Marketing Culture & Learning

"Our business is under pressure. We have no other option but to grow. And when you analyze the opportunities, particularly with women, there's nowhere to go but up. So we took a look in the mirror and decided there was a lot we could do with our marketing initiatives to become more inclusive. We are about championing people—within the company, with our partners and reflecting that approach at the consumer level.

"Our marketing team composition has shifted in the past couple of years. Our team is 50-50 male-female, with a balanced split at all levels. The new challenge is to reflect that inclusivity for our brands and in our work.

"We know there's a big gap in traditional beer marketing, and alcohol in general. So we partnered with #SeeHer so our team could have access to the right data and resources to see how we can more accurately reflect women and men in our communications and programs. We orchestrated a boot camp for our marketing team and agency partners to get comfortable with these new tools. The boot camp inspired us to recreate a few of our Budweiser print ads from the 1950s, to better represent women in a more balanced role. The result was a very successful campaign that ran on March 8, 2019, for International Women's Day that more accurately reflects women.

"I was really proud of what the team did. Fifty million impressions in one day in a print campaign? That just doesn't typically happen. So we struck a nerve in society, and for the team, we felt so empowered.

"These initiatives aren't just occurring in the U.S. Last year, AB InBev's South Africa team won a Cannes Lions Grand Prix for a campaign for Carling Black Label that addressed domestic violence."

On the left, Budweiser ads from the 1950s and 1960s; on the right, reimagined versions adapted for 2019.

In her own words: Lindsay King, Global Vice President, People Continuity

"One part of our commitment to being more inclusive and diverse throughout the business was through the development of internal mentoring and sponsorship programs.

"I had the most positive experience of being mentored by two senior men in my career, but this was not part of any formal or official AB InBev program. They both championed me through my career, and I was even promoted upon return from both of my maternity leaves. They stretched me into new levels of responsibility that I didn't think I was even close to qualified for. They pushed me out of my comfort zone and encouraged me to pursue an international career. It took me a while to realize that these types of organic relationships don't happen for all women, which is why we created a formal program.

"The AB InBev Women in Beer Global Mentoring Program ensures that our female talent pool gains the support and visibility they need to advance. An innovative toolkit delivers engaging content for both mentees and mentors.

"Management was more than willing to participate in the mentoring program once we explained its benefits: getting to know more women in the organization, sponsoring them by opening doors to new opportunities, etc. We did have to train them on how to effectively mentor, as traditionally people mentor women on soft skills and mentor men on business results. Once we had the dialogue about changing the narrative, the outcome has been very successful.

"During my time in Australia, we partnered with an external organization that did a mentorship program for the women in our business, with men and women in other organizations. We observed the way they matched people, how they formalized things, what routines they put in place and how they measured success. We used all of this as the base for our own program, put the AB InBev spin on it and learned from our mistakes as we went along.

"Just as mentoring isn't organic, neither can you accidentally hire and advance female talent. We had a plan and held ourselves accountable. Today nearly half of AB InBev's U.S. breweries and a quarter of our breweries in Argentina, China and Europe are led by female head brewmasters. These women have played a crucial role in brewing some of AB InBev's best-known products."

In her own words: Laura Brady, Global Director, Diversity & Inclusion

"As evidence of AB InBev's continuing and successful commitment to gender equality, we are proud to be the first beer company in the Bloomberg Gender-Equality Index for 2019. The index selects and highlights companies committed to transparency in gender reporting and advancing women's equality in the workplace.

"Our public commitment to gender equality is not new. In 2016, we were the first major brewer to sign up for then President Obama's Equal Pay Pledge. Since then we have conducted an annual gender pay analysis and constantly update our hiring and promotion practices to remove unconscious bias. We've just recently launched our third iteration of unconscious bias training that we call 'bias breaking,' which has taken the concept of unconscious bias to another level—giving our colleagues tangible ways to spot and intervene when they observe bias in performance review meetings.

"We've also expanded our focus for gender equality across our value chain. In South America, our Growth for a Dream program has committed to supporting 80,000 small business owners by providing business skills training and access to affordable financial products to improve their incomes and livelihoods. In Africa, AB InBev funds and mentors female barley farmers in adopting sustainable practices.

"Today our efforts on diversity and inclusion go beyond gender. We've supported LGBT rights with a variety of programs and some of our largest brands. In the U.S., Bud Light has supported the LGBT community and GLAAD for the past 20 years. In Brazil, Skol was the first beer brand to sponsor the Brazilian LGBT Pride Parade and has raised awareness of LGBT inclusion through several campaigns. In Australia, Carlton & United Breweries pledged its support for marriage equality before same-sex marriage legislation passed.

"These issues are global and affect our consumers, our employees and our partners. We will continue to innovate and replicate."

Taking action on AB InBev's experience

• If you pursue increasing the number of female consumers as a growth strategy, don't just alter the mix of marketing efforts, alter the composition of your marketing teams as well.

• Don't assume that mentors know how to mentor or sponsor women. Provide the training and tools that increase the chance of success.

• Learn from the best and commit with the best. Partner with organizations that have the experience and data that can accelerate diversity and inclusion efforts. Be public and transparent with your efforts, and earn entry into the leadership ranks.

Since President John F. Kennedy signed the Equal Pay Act of 1963, it has been illegal in the United States to pay men and women working in the same place different salaries for similar work. And yet, in 2019, on average, a woman working full-time earns 80.7 cents for every dollar a man earns.

Business Insider, April 2019:
https://www.businessinsider.com/gender-wage-pay-gap-charts-2017-3.

Skillshare
Impact Shapes Policy

Skillshare is an online learning community for creators, entrepreneurs and curious lifelong learners, with thousands of classes in creative pursuits, business, design and technology. Aimed at students of all ages, geographies or knowledge levels, Skillshare is an all-you-can-eat learning buffet that costs $15 a month or $99 a year.

CEO Matt Cooper believes that talent is equally distributed, but opportunity and education are not. Skillshare is designed to level the playing field by delivering remote learning to anyone, anywhere, at any time, at an affordable cost. But what about the company's own HR practices? For Cooper, they have to be consistent with this promise.

Skillshare effected change by:

• Mirroring the flexibility Skillshare offers students, with its employees. For example, employees have broad leeway about choosing to work from home, and 20 percent of Skillshare's workforce is remote. Employees are measured by outcomes rather than time spent at the office. These flexible policies allow Skillshare to attract a diverse roster of talent from all over the world and empower employees taking care of families, making the company and the product better as a result.

• Equally distributing opportunity to women by instituting a no-negotiation compensation policy for all, based on a grid of skill sets and not a person's ability to negotiate.

• Encouraging employees to shape their work at Skillshare around their lives and not the other way around.

* * *

In Cooper's own words

"Access to learning is our business model, and that manifests in a couple of ways. One is the subscription approach. We don't want you to have to pay more to learn more. So once you are a Skillshare member, you have access to everything we have. For a very affordable price, we deliver a lot of value to a lot of people who, whether due to economics, geography or other factors, wouldn't otherwise have access to this kind of learning. That also has significant cross-gender impact.

"Shortly after I started, we did an audit of our compensation and, sure enough, we had two people sitting next to each other doing the same job, with a 10 percent pay difference. Negotiation has an impact on compensation. If you're our general counsel, negotiation is part of your job. If you're a software engineer, negotiation has nothing to do with what we need you to do and what we're paying you for. So now we have a no-negotiation policy for our compensation.

"Basically, we have five to six levels for every role within the company that span an individual-contributor track and a management track. Depending on what level you are and what role you're in, there is a set compensation, and that's where you start. Everybody starts in the same place; there is no negotiation. It just ensures that we are not paying people for things that make it easy to get them to say yes and get them on board, but don't really impact what they're doing every day and what value they're bringing the organization.

"It's been an interesting process rolling this out over the last couple of years. There are times when we know that if we're willing to throw in another $5,000 to $10,000, we could close that candidate we really want, but we just have to sell around it. We have to sell other things. I think it has successfully accomplished the goal of making sure that everyone is getting paid the same amount for the same work.

"Another policy we rolled out, which is something I had at a previous company, is everybody can work from home on Tuesdays. In general, we're very flexible about when you work from home. Do what you need to do, be an adult, and you can have all the flexibility you want.

"I drive my daughters to volleyball on Tuesdays, otherwise I'd be on the train coming back from New Jersey. Having that flexibility allows people to schedule their lives around their work as opposed to the other way around. Particularly for working mothers, this makes life a lot easier.

"About 20 percent of our team doesn't actually work in our New York office; they work all over the place. So if we find a very talented engineer who needs to work from home for personal or family reasons, no problem. It's the impact we value, not seeing someone's face every day.

"One other policy that I think is pretty unique: We allow you to work remotely for up to a month, once a year. If you want to take your family and go live on the beach for a month or travel home and spend a month with your parents, you can work remotely for up to four weeks.

"Particularly for those of us with families, that kind of flexibility is very welcome.

"The reality is anybody can walk down the street and make more money somewhere else, especially if you are a female engineer in New York. But are you getting all the other things? Are you getting that flexibility? Are you working for a company you feel good about, that has impact? We have created a lot of things to persuade someone to come work with us. "Much of what we have done to support our employees provides opportunities that women don't find elsewhere. And these policies have been very intentional.

"We want to give everyone opportunity to progress, to grow, to learn, to develop, to have good financial outcomes, to have good personal outcomes. And I think we are. All the things we're doing within the business have been centered on how we have built this company. Ultimately these things don't happen unless someone like me at the top is reflecting it as a priority."

Taking action on Skillshare's experience

• Ensure that the values reflected in your business model translate to the way you run your workplace. Your employees have a right to expect it.

• Enact a "take it or leave it" no-negotiation policy for new hires, and manage expectations for future salary increases through a transparent grid of pay levels.

• Make it easier for someone with responsibilities at home to work remotely and be valued for what they contribute, not by how often they are in the office.

Part II
Changing Corporate Culture

Change is a process, not an event.

What the instigators in this section did was see an opportunity, plot a course, involve others, make a business case to senior management, involve still more people, measure impact, and have a bias for action.

Analyze, adjust, advance.

Women make 80 percent of purchase decisions, but only 3 percent of advertising agency creative directors are women.

The 3% Movement: https://www.3percentmovement.com/mission.

Kenneth Roman
Talent-Based Decisions in the 1960s, '70s and '80s

When Ken Roman joined advertising agency Ogilvy & Mather in 1963, there were no women in the client-facing account group, none in the research department and a handful in the media department. By the time he became CEO 22 years later, the agency had hired and promoted so many women that the issue was moot. Women were part of the culture. Roman has since retired. Back in the day, he didn't set out to push women forward, or even to change Ogilvy's historically male culture. He was simply in search of the right talent for clients like General Foods and Gillette.

Roman effected change by:

• Addressing business problems, not gender problems.

• Seeking out the best talent, without regard for gender, when hiring, promoting and compensating talent inside the agency and acting as their sponsors to open opportunities for them.

• Acting on advice from internal advocates who pushed him to innovate.

* * *

In Roman's own words

"We're talking about more than 50 years ago, when the role of women in advertising wasn't very great. It was predominantly male on both the agency and client sides.

"When I hired the first female account executive, Joanne Black, I wasn't looking for a woman—I was looking for a good account executive for Gillette Cosmetics. When that business didn't take off, Joanne went on to work on our Sears account. She then left for the client side and became the Senior Vice President Marketing at American Express.

"I wanted to be successful, and I wanted the agency to be successful. Our clients wanted great advertising. Of course, for some clients it was more acceptable to have women leading the account—like General Foods because their target customers were women. General Foods was several years behind the agency in hiring women.

"As opportunities opened up, we transferred women from those 'appropriate' accounts to far less traditionally female accounts, like Uniroyal Tires and Shell, where they were just as successful.

"Shelly Lazarus had been working on the American Express account and earning rave reviews from the client and team. When I asked her what she wanted for her next assignment, I expected her to ask to take over one of our big accounts. Instead, Shelly wanted to be transferred to our direct-marketing group, which in those days was perceived as a lesser group—it wasn't seen as the first team. I went to see the head of the group who said, 'You're just trying to get rid of one of your people.' I said, 'She's a star.' I went back three times and finally he took her. A few months later he said, 'Shelly is the best thing that ever happened to me.' Yes, I pushed and advocated as her sponsor, but the real point is that by asking to go to a smaller group, Shelly gained management experience at a much earlier age. She went on to become president of Ogilvy & Mather Direct in New York in 1989, and in 1996 became the CEO of all of Ogilvy Worldwide, operating in 130+ countries.

"In the 1980s, I was proud of the number of women moving into decision-making roles at the agency and our track record for promoting them. Elaine Reiss was head of our legal department. I promoted her to General Counsel and put her on the board as Corporate Secretary. Our Personnel Director (what we called HR back then) was Fran Devereux. Both women were highly visible and advocates for other women. It was Fran who raised our consciousness, and got us to adjust pay for women.

"And yet, the agency was slammed with an EEOC [Equal Employment Opportunity Commission] sex discrimination action, which later became a class-action suit, brought by two female officers on behalf of women officers as a class. They accused us of discriminating against women as a class and not paying them fairly. We defended that suit for 11 years, through different courts and appeals. In the end, the decision in our favor involved statistics—regression analyses, to factor in education, military service and other variables. During this period, I instructed people to treat both women fairly—no retaliation. Over the course of those 11 years, they received several raises and promotions. No other female officers volunteered to join the 'class.' When I suggested settling the suit I was told the women were against it. They felt the agency had treated them fairly and wanted to see it vindicated.

"Later I became concerned that some of our best women were, of course, having families and choosing to leave their jobs. One of them, Ann Iverson, was doing a great job for General Foods. She had a baby and I called to ask her to come back. She said, 'Well, I've got this baby.' So, and this was innovative at the time, I asked her to come back half-days. She did for several weeks, eventually came back full-time and then ended up transferring to Houston and running the huge Shell account.

"I did what I did to help women along the way as people, not as women, because I needed talent. I went to Elaine Reiss and Fran Devereux and asked what could we do to get more great people. I wasn't talking about women—just people. If I could stop some of the great people we already had from leaving, that would be one step. We promote some of our best women, I said, and just about the time they're ready to take on more responsibility, they have a family and they stay home. What do we have to do? What do they need? Elaine and Fran said, 'What about emergency daycare?'

"It turns out that professional women making a reasonable amount of money have help and didn't send their children to daycare. But what they did need was emergency daycare—when the nanny or sitter is sick or a no-show. In those days, it wasn't appropriate to bring your child to the office. So we looked at emergency daycare, and we set up a joint program with law firm Cravath, Swaine & Moore, which was in our building.

"An unsung hero for Ogilvy's track record for women's advancement was Fran Devereaux, Personnel Director. More than anyone, Fran raised our consciousness about treating women fairly—to pay them equally for equal jobs, to promote them to better accounts regardless of gender. When I discussed raises for my group with her, she would note those that needed adjustment. And when we had open positions, she would be fearless in recommending a woman.

"One day we needed a top person to handle the Uniroyal Tires account. 'What do you think about Sharon McGavin?' Fran asked. I thought

Sharon was terrific, but working with tire dealers? Fran thought we should give it a try, and Fran was right.

"Find people you trust, and act on what they advise."

Taking action on Roman's experience

• Promote talented women into nontraditional roles where they can shine. Sponsor them. Repeat and repeat again.

• Pay attention to trending issues that are causing women to leave management positions, and adapt your culture accordingly.

• Listen to women who are championing for other women. Act on their advice.

Women account for just 8 percent of all the directors of the top-grossing 250 domestic films of 2018.

Omnicom and Omniwomen
Increasing Women Leaders Globally

Yesterday's "Mad Men" ad agencies have become today's global communications and media empires, and Omnicom is the second largest in the world, with 70,000+ employees, half of whom are women.

Yet Executive Vice President Janet Riccio knew that women were still underrepresented at the top. Riccio used her convening power as Dean of Omnicom University, which provides advanced skills training for current and future leaders, to launch Omniwomen and elevate women in greater numbers.

In only five years, Omniwomen has become a proven catalyst to increase the influence and number of senior women leaders and now operates chapters in 15 markets around the world, including China.

The Omniwomen initiative is effecting change by:

• Providing opportunities for women to come together in person for orchestrated, candid conversations at special events, panels and training sessions.

• Placing mentorship at the center of its programming, and following on with sponsorship.

• Transferring what succeeded in one geographic location to another, with a resulting global footprint.

* * *

In Riccio's own words

"In 2014, I launched Omniwomen with one mission in mind: to serve as a catalyst to increase the influence and number of senior women leaders throughout Omnicom globally. From the outset, women around the world started raising their hands asking for an Omniwomen chapter within their country, their region or their city. Today we have 15 chapters around the world from China to Chicago to London to New York.

"Mentorship programs and mentoring events have become staples within each chapter's tool box. Whether it's speed-mentoring events, as we have done in Chicago and Germany, or highly structured mentor-mentee programs underway in the U.K. and France, all our chapter leaders recognize the importance of mentorship.

"Mentors advise you, and sponsors advocate for you, and we came to the early realization that women need both. We introduced a number of events exclusively centered on sponsorships. For Omniwomen to achieve its mission, we needed to build the confidence of our very talented women to have the important conversations with their bosses about promotion, about compensation and about career paths. We are a global enterprise in 130+ countries, and one of the priceless outcomes is how sponsors give women access to their own Omnicom network so they can make new connections.

"Each Omniwomen chapter undertakes mentorship and sponsorship in their own unique way, tailored to the needs of their constituency, and we are seeing very tangible results.

"Omniwomen San Francisco hosted the event 'From Mentorship to Sponsorship,' which featured a panel discussion of five women from different Bay Area Omnicom agencies sharing stories of how mentors and sponsors helped them achieve their career success.

"Omniwomen Chicago created mentoring rounds that mimicked speed dating, connecting women throughout the Omnicom network with members of the chapter to learn about empowering women in the workforce. On International Women's Day in 2018, Omniwomen Chicago also ran mentorship breakout sessions led by Preeti Nadgar, one of the agency's most visible female client strategists.

"Omniwomen D.C. replicated Chicago's speed-mentoring event in honor of International Women's Day. The event hosted dozens of Omnicom agency colleagues who gathered to find a mentor and learn more about the other agencies within the Omnicom family.

"Speed mentoring then crossed borders when Omniwomen Germany hosted a 'Speed Dating Mentoring Event' and gathered 32 mentors, including 15 very senior managing directors of Omnicom agencies.

"In Shanghai, Omniwomen held an event to inspire and celebrate female staff across the Omnicom network in Greater China. Unveiled during the event was a campaign developed by our TBWA Shanghai agency using real testimonials where women shared their stories on how their personal passions are reflected in their professional lives. This was followed by a panel discussion with the women featured in the campaign, and the announcement of a series of upcoming career-nurturing initiatives to bring together female talent in an open and supportive environment for sharing, networking and learning.

"Omniwomen has indeed been a catalyst for change. The number of women being promoted into Omnicom senior leadership roles is on the rise. For the first time ever, a woman has been named CEO of one of our global creative agencies, CEO of one of our global communications agencies and CEO of one of our global media companies.

"Omniwomen is a source of pride across Omnicom. We believe we attract talented women to Omnicom because of it, and we keep talented women within Omnicom as a result of it.

"With over 70,000 employees, half of whom are women, we consider every Omnicom employee to be a part of Omniwomen."

Taking action on Omniwomen's experience

• Give non-HQ offices a safe space to innovate and make a women's advocacy program their own. Transfer creative ideas from market to market, but tailor to local needs and concerns.

• Deploy both mentorship and sponsorship components.

• Personalize the digital world by providing opportunities to participate at in-person, candid events, which builds credibility and a visible enthusiasm that sparks momentum.

ZS Associates
Forecasting First and Then Aiming Higher

A professional services firm like ZS might have opted to leverage its women's initiative to focus primarily on individual career journeys. Instead, the 6,000+ men and women that comprise this global consulting firm have mobilized in support of an ambitious vision of achieving 50-50 representation of women across the firm.

ZS's Women's Leadership Initiative (WLI) encourages all ZS people to 'bring your whole self to work,' a mantra that serves as a guiding principle and encourages women to be direct and transparent about what they want for their own journeys. The WLI is the catalyst behind the 50-50 vision, and Principal Hensley Evans is a key force in championing it. Evans is the first woman hired from outside ZS at the Principal level and currently leads the Patient and Consumer Health practice.

The WLI is effecting change by:

• Gaining alignment among the firm's top management on a vision of 50-50 representation of women at ZS. This ambitious vision serves as a "North Star" and is critical to making measurable progress.

• Implementing key initiatives focused on hiring, engagement and retention—HER, for short.

• Providing a formal one-year mentorship program for every woman who joins at, or is promoted to, the manager level so that she receives coaching, forges connections and has a forum for seeking advice and sharing challenges.

* * *

In Evans' own words

"I can't take credit for forming the Women's Leadership Initiative at ZS because it existed for five years prior to my joining the firm. Before I accepted the offer from ZS though, I did ask questions to understand who the women leaders were and subsequently encouraged ZS to make those leaders visible.

"Upon joining, I met several women leaders and became involved in the WLI. Having worked in other organizations, I think I brought a fresh perspective that helped us build on the foundation previous WLI leaders laid and help continue the WLI's progress.

"ZS is a privately held firm and has evidenced its commitment to the WLI by creating a Women's Leadership Advisory Board. Over time we've expanded the participation on that advisory board to include not only women, but men and allies who will help support our objectives of making our organization a great place for women and all people at ZS to join and grow their professional careers.

"Our challenges, from a female representation standpoint, aren't that we're not attracting young women to join us out of undergrad or MBA programs. We're close to 50 percent representation of women at those levels already. The real issue is that our attrition rate for women is just a little bit higher than that of men at every level. The fact that our experienced hires at the manager level and above are more male, despite various recruiting efforts aimed at ensuring that ZS is considering a diverse pool of candidates, compounds the issue. The cumulative result is that there are fewer women at the leadership level than there are men.

"As part of the process of improving women's representation at senior levels, we looked at other global consulting organizations to understand how they are addressing these issues. Many have specific representation goals, and several even set a timeline for achieving those, but we found every one of them was aiming lower than 50 percent representation.

"ZS is a very analytical organization. We created a forecast model that looked at our existing data, looked at our existing attrition rates and asked, 'If we take x and y actions, what could we attain by 2020? What can we get to by 2025?' After examining historical and existing data, setting an objective that was anything less than the relative proportions in the population seemed arbitrary.

"One of the key things that gave us the courage to establish a vision of achieving 50-50 representation among men and women is the support of the men on the advisory board. It made sense to them. Women make up 50 percent of the population; why wouldn't we be 50 percent of the organization, and 50 percent of the leadership?

"Capitalizing on this initial support, we embarked on a yearlong process leading up to the global rollout of the 50-50 vision, which required clear communication, patience and unwavering commitment.

"During this time, we had conversations with several members of senior leadership at ZS. We solicited feedback from a variety of people in different roles and in different geographies.

"We didn't need a forecasting model to tell us is that if attrition of women is even a tiny bit higher than that of men, we need to increase the funnel to bring in more qualified women candidates for open positions at the manager level and above. So we're working to implement a variety of initiatives that will attract diverse candidates to ZS and drive retention.

"As part of the effort to understand the difference in our retention of men and women, we looked at our annual employee engagement survey to see if there were specific areas where scores for women were lower than those of men. Our hope is that the data in the survey may provide us with additional insights that further inform our efforts to improve women's engagement in the firm—increasing the sense of belonging here.

"ZS operates 23 offices in 12 countries. Globally, we work to build a culture we describe as a 'caring meritocracy' reflecting respect, support, flexibility and connections. These qualities are especially important to women over the course of their career and the reason why many choose ZS as the place to build their professional life.

"Because of my leadership role, and as a woman, I feel the responsibility of living the mantra 'Bring your whole self to work.' I share my personal calendar with the entire organization, and I include appointments such as 'morning run,' 'family time' and 'drop Kaia at soccer practice.' I share how I am managing my work, health and family commitments. I work from Europe, so I often take conference calls with colleagues in the evening from home, and I've definitely paused a conference call so I can answer a question for my daughter. I do block my calendar at specific times so I can get some quality time with my family.

"I don't always find the right balance, and I believe that if I only share the successes, I may make it harder for other women to believe that they can pursue leadership roles and have a family and personal life. I hope that by letting people see that in addition to focusing on work, I make time for and prioritize my family—and myself—they will feel permission to find their own ways to do the same. I know that many ZSers—no matter their gender identity—appreciate the example I am trying to set.

"Laura Elisa Montealegre and Sara Burbine co-lead the New York office's WLI. Their team includes both female and male advocates who strive to ensure that ZS women feel welcomed, supported and empowered at work. After speaking with the women in the office about their needs, Laura and Sara decided to focus the local initiative on three areas: increasing opportunities for mentorship and networking for women, increasing professional development opportunities for women, and increasing officewide understanding of women's issues. With these goals in mind, one of the most successful workshops helped ZS employees in the New York office understand how to be allies and support their women coworkers.

"I love this testimonial from Jen Tedaldi, a ZSer in the New York office: 'The WLI helps women realize that you can authentically be yourself and still be a leader. Actually, that you can be the best type of leader when you are true to who you are and use your skills to inspire other people.'

"Imagine how freeing that is, to be your authentic self at work!"

Taking action on the ZS/WLI experience

• Set a "North Star" women's strategy that is embraced by the men and women at the highest level of the firm.

• Use data to understand attrition rates and what needs to change in hiring and retention practices.

• Identify and empower a visible and respected role model who is fearless in revealing how she balances, and sometimes doesn't balance, work and home.

Part III
Overcoming Obstacles Through Systemic Change

Every woman doesn't need to break the glass ceiling. She just needs to bend it to her advantage.

The innovative mentors on the following pages found workarounds to accelerate progress for others, or they created an entirely new model to bypass typical barriers.

Women make up 45 percent of law firm associates but only 23 percent of partners and 19 percent of equity partners.

Lori Silva
Consistently Advocating for Change

Lori Silva went into culture shock in her early 30s. Until then, she had only worked at trade-show businesses run by women. It was only when she joined a business exclusively run by men that she knew she had the benefit of an experience that wasn't normal for most women. Soon thereafter, Silva realized she had an obligation to mentor the women on her new team and within the broader organization, as well as to educate senior management on the need for gender diversity.

Twenty-plus years later, Silva is Managing Director, Advanced Manufacturing Group, at Informa Markets, part of the world's largest B2B events organizer. She is responsible for the operational, profit and loss, and strategic direction of the business. Silva is committed to getting the best from organizations, developing talent, and remaining an active role model and advocate for women advancing their careers.

Silva effected change by:

• Crafting and communicating effective mentoring initiatives that support the goals of the senior management team.

- Seeking out influential, senior male mentors for herself.

- Mentoring women and girls outside of her professional work.

＊＊

In Silva's own words

"Helping women move forward in their careers and gain leadership roles is a huge passion of mine and encompasses just about every aspect of my life, even outside of business. I am active in programs like 'Girls on the Run,' which inspires girls to be joyful, healthy and confident. The program envisions a world where every girl knows and activates her limitless potential and is free to boldly pursue her dreams.

"I worked at a woman-owned business when my career began, followed by a family-run business with the daughter at the head. She was a mentor and, best of all, an incredibly strong woman. It wasn't until I was in my early 30s that I worked at a company run exclusively by male executives—no females. That was a shock to the system. I realized I had been in a bubble that wasn't normal and did not mirror most women's experience. That's when I decided that we needed to educate men and mentor women to level the playing field.

"I've always been on the operating side of the businesses where I worked—not in HR. So when I was appointed the global lead for UBM's gender diversity program in mid-2017 [UBM was acquired by Informa in 2018], it felt a bit overwhelming. I thought, what does that mean? I wasn't quite sure it was something I could do along with managing the business. I spent some time with the CEO, Tim Cobbold, who shared personal stories about his mother, who was a single working mother, and her struggles. I also spoke to Dame Helen Alexander, UBM's board chairman and the first female president of the Confederation of British Industry. She was focused on championing women leaders and was quite impressive. I went outside of the UBM network and met with the heads of gender diversity at Burberry and the BBC (among others) to understand how they implemented their programs, and combed through piles of published research materials.

"With all that due diligence, I developed our program with a mission to improve gender diversity at a leadership level, advance women leaders and position UBM as the employer of choice. The key drivers of the program are focused on recruitment, development, compensation and community. That work has been a major highlight for me. The program, while in its infancy, has been well received, and I'm excited to see the future impact on our business. We also launched the 'Empower Women's Leaders' program a few years ago, where I executed a global summer tour around our offices to speak about women in leadership and shared my own journey. Women told us this helped them better cope with the challenges and roadblocks they were facing.

"Because a large part of Informa's business is international exhibitions, I have a terrific platform to instigate change outside of our organization. We do a lot of events, and one of the other programs we put together is organized gatherings in a live setting. One of our initiatives is focused on engineering. We bring together women in engineering, and we promote to the broader engineering world the importance of women leaders in the engineering environment.

"For the past couple of years, I've been serving on the SISO [the Society for Independent Show Organizers] Women Special Interest Group, helping to develop program content for the SISO Executive Women's Forum and the SISO Women's Leadership Conference. Both programs are focused on networking, peer support and helping to develop leadership skills for women in the events industry. Combined, these events attract 100 women annually and growing.

"When I've looked for mentors for myself, I look for a balance. I have a very strong influential male mentor in my world right now. He is a CEO in a large global organization. He has a high level of emotional intelligence and focuses on driving women's initiatives in his organization. I sought him out because I thought he could be a great mentor for me as I move our programs forward.

"Men also have a crucial role to play in educating the public about women leaders. Progress is born from both men and women promoting and sponsoring female leaders."

Taking action on Silva's experience

• To effect change within an organization, tap into senior managements' personal experiences about women leaders and gender diversity.

• Look outside your organization and industry for inspiration and even a mentor who can provide a new perspective.

• Seek roles at women-run or women-led organizations to influence broader change.

Kristy Wallace
The Nuts and Bolts of Making
Change Happen

Every idea needs landing gear as well as wings. Kristy Wallace has developed three key mentoring programs as the CEO of the Ellevate Network and drives the overall strategy and vision of an organization redefining how women network in the digital age.

If Ellevate's mission is to change the culture of business from the inside out by providing professional women with the community they need to take the next step in their careers, Wallace's role is to make it happen with tangible programs that resonate with its membership.

In her career, Wallace has had plenty of experience driving systemic change from the inside out. At one company, she advocated for a maternity policy where none had existed. After a merger with another company, she became an advocate for diversity when she was the only woman on the senior management team. Through it all, Wallace has had a bias for action.

Wallace effected change by:

• Ensuring that leadership teams commit to change not just programs.

• Simplifying mentoring programs to focus on making deeper connections, removing barriers to success and helping women get the advice and support they need to advance.

• Harnessing the power of women who want to see more women move forward, assume leadership, run businesses and launch businesses.

***

In Wallace's own words

"The greatest impact I have had upending the status quo is through my work at Ellevate. We are focused on changing the culture of business from the inside out. We support women across multiple organizations to achieve success but also help them identify and remove the systemic barriers that are keeping them back. Discussing our point of view and presenting thought leadership to senior management at major corporations guides them ultimately to greater diversity and a better workplace.

"Oftentimes mentoring programs become so complex that you miss the point of why mentoring is so important in the first place, which is making deeper connections aimed at helping others get the advice and support they need to move forward.

"Ellevate has three key initiatives: our Leadership Luncheons, Mentoring Meetups and our Squads program.

"Leadership Luncheons bring together senior women for issue processing and business development. As we all know, women are scarce at the top. At major companies, women represent only 17 percent of leadership. When it comes to the Fortune 500, that number sinks even lower; female CEOs lead only 5 percent of Fortune 500 companies. Leadership Luncheons provide a space for women in those positions to come together, support each other and bond into a community that provides opportunities to grow their businesses as well.

"Ellevate's Mentoring Meetups are like speed dating for mentoring. Women come and identify themselves either as a mentor or a mentee. It doesn't matter what stage you are in your career, you get to choose what role you play each time. We all need a little mentoring sometimes, and other times we feel a little bit more confident giving advice. There's always a set topic, so we're really focused on the issue we want to address. During the event, a mentee will go and meet with five to seven different mentors. She will ask each for advice on the same issue, the same problem, the same opportunity, and during the event she will get different perspectives, viewpoints and advice. The aim is to focus on short-term actionable goals. We're not planning where you're going to be in five or 10 years. Our goal is identifying how to deal with a particular issue and what you are going to do every single day to keep moving forward. Everyone leaves with buckets of ideas and guidance.

"Our Squads program is an online community of six to eight women at similar stages in their careers from different geographies. They commit to a half-hour a week for 12 weeks via online video chat to discuss a set curriculum. They are women at similar stages, who might be in different industries, different functions and different regions. The power of the conversation is the diversity of thought. Our measurement surveys tell us that at the end of the 12 weeks, the women are 80 percent more confident in taking the next step in their career.

"We've had several women who have signed up for multiple cohorts of Squads because they've found it so powerful and a great accountability tool for ongoing, regular weekly touchpoints with others. We've also had women whose Squads continue to meet even after the 12 weeks. I met someone last week who told me that every quarter, three of them continue to meet up in person even though they are in Boston, New York and Connecticut. Another woman said that someone from her Squad who is based in California was coming to speak at Harvard, and she called her up to ask if she could stay with her. 'It's great! I have a virtual friend that is staying with me in real life!'

"The issues we are trying to address is how do we foster these relationships of support aimed at professional development? And we know that there isn't always a clear line between business and personal life. That's why it's really important to get the support, the advice and the insights we all need to navigate these personal and professional decisions."

Taking action on Wallace's experience

• Be mentor-ambidextrous. Sometimes you are a mentee and sometimes you are a mentor. At different points in our career, we either need to seek advice or have the confidence to share advice.

• Join a network that is a safe space to discuss issues and find support, making sure it is a successful framework with an orchestrator that keeps the momentum going.

• Keep it simple and without entanglements. Try speed mentoring inside your business or industry to gain different expert perspectives with fewer long-term commitments.

Laura Barger
Intervening at Critical Tipping Points

In her role at global retained executive search firm Raines International, Laura Barger mentors the young women she hires so that they have the best opportunities to succeed. Barger's own mentoring path began while she was a student at the University of Pennsylvania, where she volunteered for a community program that taught supplemental health education to fifth-grade girls.

Today she is on the Young Leadership Board for America Needs You, a nonprofit that fights for the economic mobility of low-income first-generation college students, and serves as one of its mentor coaches.

Barger effected change by:

• Offering girls and women guidance at critical junctures in their path forward, when they are facing tough challenges head-on.

• Addressing issues of confidence and positive self-image at the grade-school level.

• Identifying at-risk cohorts—i.e., low-income, first-generation college students—at the university level and intervening early.

• Actively working with new hires to accelerate their success.

* * *

In Barger's own words

"I didn't realize how important it was for fifth graders to see someone other than their parents and teachers be a youthful voice of guidance for them. Having a college student in the classroom with them really changed their perspective on what they could be when they grew up.

"In order to foster a better self-image, my fellow student-teachers and I asked the girls to write down positive adjectives about themselves. At the end of the exercise, each one stood up saying things like, 'I am funny. I am creative. I am smart.' And you could see just how empowering it was for those fifth-grade girls to speak these affirmations.

"I've been out of college for four years now. Using the skills I've learned at Raines International for what makes a good career trajectory, I work with sophomore college students in the America Needs You program and walk them through the decisions they need to think about and the choices they need to make to get to the place they want to go.

"Fifty percent of the 'fellows' I mentor are women, and during the course of the program the change in their confidence and belief in their ability is evident. The support system is holistic and the mentor-coach relationships typically follow the students through graduation, internships and the beginning of their work careers.

"At Raines International, we didn't have a formal mentorship program when I joined, so I made my own rule: You have to help the people who are coming in, and you have to advance them at a quicker rate rather than expecting them to figure it out on their own and sink or swim.

"When my CEO asks me, 'Who do you think we should be promoting?' I have the position of power to say, 'You have to look at Madison or Allison.' And when he pushes back saying, 'They're not even recruiters yet,' I tell him to give them the opportunity because they can hack it. That's the kind of incredible experience I've had here and the opportunity to really raise people up and be a positive influence in their careers.

"If I'm the person who hired another woman into our organization, then I'm also the person who is responsible for making sure that she succeeds here and we retain her."

Taking action on Barger's experience

• Support programs at grade school and college levels that help build knowledge, skills and confidence. Girls need role models outside of their parents and teachers.

• After hiring a new employee, don't wait until she is floundering to offer assistance. Introduce her early to formal or informal mentoring. Her success enhances yours.

• Whether you're a man or a woman, make sure you are advocating for high-potential people in closed-door meetings. This kind of sponsorship can create successful career trajectories for women from the beginning of their careers to executive-level positions.

One in five firms with revenue of $1 million
or more is woman-owned.

AmericanExpress OPEN, "The State of Women-Owned Businesses 2017."

Fran Pastore
The Confidence Solution

When Fran Pastore launched the Women's Business Development Council (WBDC) in Connecticut in 1997, she was a 36-year-old single mother with 4-year-old and 7-year-old daughters. Today WBDC has moved 14,000+ women toward economic equity by providing them with tools, mentoring and services in entrepreneurial training, financial education and access to working capital. Pastore is widely regarded as a champion for women, families and communities throughout Connecticut.

Pastore attributes her success to the early support and mentorship of several women in her life, including Bpeace's own Toni Maloney who helped her fulfill a personal career goal by inviting her to travel to Rwanda in 2010. Pastore had decided to add international experience to her skills, so she volunteered as a Skillanthropist with the Business Council for Peace (Bpeace) and traveled to Rwanda to train and mentor a group of genocide survivors who were starting the country's first ice-cream store. As a result of that experience, she is now a sought-after international champion focused on building ecosystems to support women entrepreneurs.

The U.S. Department of State has called on her to train women entrepreneurs in Costa Rica, and she has represented the U.S. in Turkey and Ethiopia. Pastore has also testified multiple times before the U.S. Congress and was instrumental in the passage of legislation benefiting women entrepreneurs.

Through all her work with women entrepreneurs over the past 22+ years, Pastore sees one constant that holds women back: lack of confidence.

Pastore effected change by:

• Fostering self-confidence, which leads to risk-taking—an essential component of entrepreneurship.

• Providing access to working capital for women.

• Developing a strong network of supportive business owners so female entrepreneurs can find support and sponsorship.

* * *

In Pastore's own words

"I get so much pleasure and satisfaction out of helping other women achieve their goals because I had so many women help me along my path. I know how important it is to have someone who restores your confidence and believes in you, because the biggest threat to a woman's success is a lack of confidence. I see it every day in my work at WBDC. It doesn't matter how young or old a woman is—without confidence she won't take business risks, and entrepreneurship by its very nature is risky.

"Here is just one example: I met Amy when she was working at an Ivy League university in a very prestigious role but surrounded by men and constrained by gender bias issues. She had so much potential but not enough belief in her abilities. We met up informally every few months and she would share with me her struggles to progress. I encouraged her to think about running her own business, but she wasn't ready yet. Finally, two years ago, she called to tell me that she had taken the plunge and was going to run her own medical device startup. The device is now in the approval process at the FDA, and that's a big, big deal. And, full circle, she was asked by JP Morgan Chase to write a report on the impact of women entrepreneurs and their challenges and opportunities.

"Confidence can propel a woman through the many hurdles of finding partners or financing or developing technical skills. Women need confidence in themselves and the competencies necessary to take their business to the next level.

"At WBDC we offer women the opportunity to achieve both. Through classes in business essentials, accounting, sales and marketing, etc., the positive outcome we strive to achieve is for each client to develop the competencies she needs to understand not only her passion for her business, but to develop the confidence in technical business skills so she can take the leaps and risks necessary to start or grow a business. WBDC also provides a network of proven business owners who often sponsor up-and-comers by helping them access vendors and markets.

"I knew Connecticut really well, and my board thought I should gain some international experience. Through the nonprofit, Business Council for Peace, I had the opportunity to work with a group of women who were opening Rwanda's first-ever ice-cream shop. In the post-genocide era in Rwanda, there were more women entrepreneurs stepping forward but with little training and certainly no access to capital. This endeavor required both. Blue Marble Dreams, a Brooklyn-based nonprofit, provided the capital. Bpeace provided the training to 17 Rwandan women in customer service, business management and personal finance.

"The women in many cases had received very little formal education, and now they were going to be entrepreneurs. Inzozi Nziza's doors opened in June 2010. Since then, this shop has brought together dozens of Rwandan women from both sides of the 1994 genocide and equipped them with training, jobs and a sustainable income. It has also supported local farmers and producers, bolstered the local economy and provided the community with a welcoming place to gather, connect and heal. What Blue Marble and Bpeace provided was tangible; what I believe that mentors like others and me inspired was the confidence to reach for the stars.

"The WBDC has been around for 22 years. And I've had the opportunity to leverage what we've learned through that time in Connecticut building women-owned businesses, and translate it to countries like Rwanda and Costa Rica.

"Recently, with the spur of entrepreneurial activity around the globe, the landscape in Connecticut changed and WBDC's funding was at risk. As CEO, I had to work very closely with my team, state leaders and members of the WBDC Board of Directors to convey WBDC's value proposition in a new way to multiple stakeholders. The competition was fierce as the landscape had dramatically changed for services to entrepreneurs. We overcame that, but it was really the first time in my experience as the founder of WBDC that we came up against obstacles and challenges.

"At first I was angry, but then I said we are just going to keep doing what we are doing really well—because I had the confidence of knowing what works and, at the time, over a decade of experience to prove it."

Taking action on Pastore's experience

• Entrepreneurship, all over the world, is a path for women to achieve economic freedom.

• If you become an advisor, instructor or mentor to a woman entrepreneur, perhaps the most valuable outcome you can produce is increasing her confidence.

• Take what you learn as a mentor and magnify your impact, by sequentially mentoring many women over your career.

In academia, women have earned the most doctorates for eight consecutive years but are only 32 percent of full professors and 30 percent of college presidents.

Part IV
Boosting a Woman's Power to Advocate

In the end, any woman or girl needs to push her own self forward.

What advocates can do is give them the opportunity to learn from role models, to network and to access tools that increase their confidence.

As recently as 2016, 43 percent of the 150 highest-earning public companies in Silicon Valley had no female executive officers.

Liz Smith
The Multiplier Effect of Paying It Forward

Liz Smith began her career as a schoolteacher. Today, as the Senior Managing Director at global asset management firm AllianceBernstein, Smith is recognized as one of the most senior and accomplished women in the financial services industry, not only for her professional accomplishments but also her tireless support of women in finance.

Smith says the road for women in business is tough enough, and when women believe they have to do it on their own, they slow themselves down. At the same time, Smith says, you can't expect anyone to help you if you're not offering them something first or in return.

"Legendary" is how hundreds of women describe Smith. She makes sure that the women around her at all career levels also have a front-row seat to her carefully curated network.

Smith effected change by:

• Approaching every request for advice as an opportunity to advance, support and advocate for that woman, while also showing her how to do it for herself.

• Proactively arranging diversity and women's advancement seminars with the best speakers, career coaches and writers to inspire and educate women.

• Persuading women in the early stages of their education and career development, to join professional development programs to develop the skills and confidence they will need later in their careers.

***

In Smith's own words

"My work and life philosophy has been: You can't expect someone to do something for you if you've never done anything for them. I developed my book of business by forming relationships, finding out what people's needs were and helping them achieve their goals. This naturally translated into mentoring and advocating for women. What makes us rich are the relationships we develop throughout our career—our most valuable possession.

"Every woman must be responsible for helping other women because we can't do it alone. It's the small things we do collectively that make us stronger and help women advance.

"Complementing my work at AllianceBernstein is my women's network. We are a group of sales professionals from different organizations—technically competitors—who have joined together to address topics and issues of importance to women. We invite our friends—those who are younger, as well as seasoned professionals—some clients, some prospects, to get together to talk about issues such as how to get on a corporate board and pay parity. Recently we had Amanda Grant, an executive search professional, talk about negotiating skills. There were about 30 people in the room when she relayed the story of how a job with a certain salary range was offered to a woman at a lower salary range. The reason? 'That was the salary she asked for.'

"Many women don't ask for what they want. They don't use powerful language. Why apologize for having a contradictory point of view? Why say sorry for interrupting? Why say 'I will try' instead of saying 'I will.' Some women don't present themselves with a stance or physical presence that projects confidence. Sometimes you just need to make a woman aware of these things. In one case, I encouraged a woman to dress for the position she wanted. She ultimately was promoted, moved to more senior roles at several other firms and is now a recognized success in this industry.

"You think you are underpaid or not being paid fairly? Ask for what you want. You think you deserve a particular promotion? Show them why and ask for it. And use words with power, the power to persuade and lead. If you wait to be asked, your time may never come.

"For every woman I have worked with to achieve their goals, I hope they will do the same for another woman. Pay it forward.

"My favorite times are events where I interact with other women: women who manage challenging client situations, women who manage portfolios they have created, women who have started their own venture capital firms. It is because of the obstacles women face and overcome, that they are incredible and inspiring.

"When I work with young women, even students, I tell them why it is such an advantage to be a woman. We are perceptive and thoughtful. We can read a room and are able to understand the people we're dealing with so we can position ourselves accordingly.

"I'm on the board of the New York Chapter of the National Association of Security Professionals (NASP) and its foundation, which provides financial education and mentoring for talented minority high school students. We also provide assistance in the college application process, teaching them interview skills, resume writing and how to apply for financial aid. We offer college tours and personal guidance to help them get into their top school. One of the women who participated in the program and interned with AllianceBernstein, was able to get into NYU and upon graduation was offered a position at LinkedIn in Silicon Valley.

"I was an advocate for working with the mentorship program, 'Girls Who Invest,' here at AllianceBernstein. Seema Hingorani, the former CIO of New York City Retirement Systems, started this program. It offers investment management courses to female college students at Penn State and Notre Dame. At investment firms like AllianceBernstein, it also provides the opportunity to work directly with an analyst or a portfolio manager. Last year we extended an offer to one of these women for a full-time investment position.

"When we make another woman successful, she makes us all successful."

Taking action on Smith's experience

• Respond to a request for advice, or reach out to another woman at your firm or elsewhere, on how to advance in the business or industry. Offer to be a mentor, and work with her to help achieve her goal.

• How's your own presence? How's your language? What changes do you need to make to project confidence and leadership?

• Invite a group of women outside of your workplace to talk about advancement. Was it productive? Do you see it growing over time?

Mary Stutts
A Necessary Journey

Don't have a mentor? Can't find a mentor? Mary Stutts has the answers in her book, "The Missing Mentor: Women Advising Women on Power, Progress and Priorities." With hard-learned techniques and lessons from her own mentors, Stutts' book serves as a surrogate mentor to anybody who needs one.

Stutts has personally mentored and advocated for women in her role as communications leader at some of the largest companies in the U.S., including Genentech, Kaiser, Comcast and Stanford Health Care—where she currently serves as the Chief Diversity, Inclusion & Health Equity Officer.

Stutts' credibility earns her coveted speaking opportunities at panels and conferences with Fortune 500 companies. Her most important theme for women: Set clear goals for personal development and take risks.

Stutts effected change by:

• Removing any mystery about, or access to, mentoring by making her techniques and advice on career advancement available to everyone in her book.

• Inspiring and provoking audiences in corporate America via conferences, panels and seminars about diversity, career planning and advancement.

• Intercepting women and girls before they start working by aligning herself with nonprofit organizations that are advocating for women and girls—for example, How Women Lead, SHE-CAN, CSweetener and many more.

* * *

In Stutts' own words

"This journey we're all on to help women advance and truly live in the power that we have collectively and individually, is not only a noble journey, it is a necessary journey. Our future depends on it—not just the future of our households or our kids, but of our country and of the world. It is women who are going to make the difference so that we get this world literally back on the right path.

"The highlight of my career has been the opportunity to mentor so many incredible men and women, whether they reported to me, were on my team or whom I met as I was out speaking and participating in events for the different corporations where I've worked. But certainly the women really resonated with me, because no matter where they were in their career, I felt like I had been there. That was the light-bulb moment when I realized that all the stuff I went through building my career was not in vain. I can use that experience to help others make their way through it and give them the confidence that there is a path for you, and you can do it.

"Writing the book is probably the single most important action I've taken to move groups of women forward. When I'm working in the corporate world, my focus is on moving the whole company forward and growing the business. But writing the book, 'The Missing Mentor: Women Advising Women on Power, Progress and Priorities,' has had even more impact because it opened doors for me to speak at major Fortune 500 companies like Pfizer and Medtronic, at places where I worked like Genentech and others, and at conferences and diversity council meetings.

"In the Bay Area in California, I also work with the organization, How Women Lead. California recently passed legislation mandating that publicly traded companies have at least one woman on the board, and by 2021 at least two. This has inspired a new series of How Women Lead development programs to prepare women to be board members. First we bring in women who are already board members as role models. Then I work with participants in the program on their value proposition and helping them understand how to talk about yourself as a prospective board member versus applying for a regular job.

"When I mentor people, my biggest focus is putting a career development plan in place. I conduct lots of career development workshops for different organizations. It never ceases to amaze me that when I ask people, 'Raise your hand if you have a career development plan,' less than 20 percent of the men and women in the room raise their hand. I always say, if you don't know where you're going, how will you know when you've arrived? Where do you want to be in the next three years, five years, 10 years? It's a simple question, and it's essential to have an answer before you can develop a plan for advancing your career and your life and moving forward.

"SHE-CAN is a nonprofit that accesses full-ride college scholarships for young women from post-conflict countries, who return home after graduation to become changemakers in their countries. I have been mentoring a young woman who had graduated from college and was in her first job. I took her to several of the SHE-CAN activities, and she goes to any events where I am speaking.

"At one of my women's empowerment events that I do through my non-profit, TCEL (The Excellent Life Center), people were asked to share their work experiences. She came up and shared the story about her first job out of college. Her immediate boss was not treating her fairly compared with the rest of the team and she had received some negative feedback from him. Meanwhile she had heard me talk in general about that whole concept of know when to fold 'em, when to move on and when to stay and deal with the situation. So she talked about weighing the pros and cons and her decision to tell her boss she was leaving. She wasn't aware of it, but the boss's own boss thought she was doing a great job. When he found out she wanted to leave, he intervened and said, 'No, we don't want you to leave, we're going to give you a promotion, a bonus and stock.' And they promoted her over her former boss, which was just divine justice!

"Obviously there must have been something going on that the company was aware of because that's kind of unusual to do. But the point is that she went through the exercise of evaluating her options to make a logical decision, not an emotional one. She then ended up taking a year off to go to graduate school and invited me to attend her graduation in May. Now she's being recruited by all these amazing companies like Facebook and Amazon because she left that job to focus on getting her graduate degree.

"These are the stories that keep me buoyed up to do more of what I am doing to move women forward."

Taking action on Stutts' experience

• Promote or publish stories, blogs or podcasts of your own career success and creditability to influence others to advance diversity and inclusiveness.

• Help a woman develop a career development plan, or seek a mentor to help create your own plan.

• Start the journey to earn a board or leadership role for yourself by participating in training at organizations with a track record for placement.

The smallest pay gaps for women are in lower-wage professions, such as food preparation and serving workers, where women earn 99 cents on the dollar, followed by writers/authors and pharmacists, where women earn 98 percent of what their male counterparts make.

American Association of University Women, 2018.

Melissa Hartzell
Transferring Advocacy and Access

Melissa Hartzell had planned to attend college but out of financial necessity went into the workforce as a single mother. In 1995, she started her career as a receptionist. Today she is Vice President, Senior Credit Officer, at Investors Bank.

As Hartzell worked her way up the corporate ladder without a mentor of her own, she found she was not only advocating for herself but became a role model for other women. She began to informally mentor some of them on how to champion for themselves, negotiate promotions and raises, and make their voices heard. Some of those women are now managers, assistant vice presidents and vice presidents.

Two years ago, with a track record of 20+ years in banking, Hartzell, along with the Investors Bank Women's Leadership Council (WLC), decided that Investors Bank needed a formal mentoring program. Working with the Executive Vice President of Human Resources, they launched the Mentorship Pilot Program, which today has 27 mentor-mentee teams. The EVP of HR provided convincing proof of the benefits of inclusion and diversity, and the WLC has executive management's full support. Further evidence of those benefits was the bank's promotion of its first four women to Executive Vice President in 2018.

Hartzell effected change by:

• Transferring what she learned from advocating for herself, to other women.

• Demonstrating by example how to make your voice heard.

• Formalizing mentorships so that women across the organization have equal access.

* * *

In Hartzell's own words

"When I first started in financial services 20+ years ago, it was a male-dominated industry. I needed to change the culture, not just for myself, but for all the other women in the industry. I started advocating for all of us, and mentoring some of them to advocate for themselves, in order to get promotions. I'm proud to say a lot of those women are now managers, AVPs and VPs because they had a mentor and role model.

"I mentor women formally and informally. I help whoever I can because I didn't have a mentor. So for me, the higher up the ladder I go, the more I want to give back and continue to build women up.

"When we were trying to establish the Women's Leadership Council, I was so grateful to the EVP of HR because she really pushed to get senior management's support. Now that we have rolled out, the executives realize this is absolutely something they need and they are behind us 150 percent. They are now an integral part of our support network.

"I think it is really important to share my story with other women so they know that it is not easy, and we all struggle. Every one of us has a story, and the story makes us who we are today. So we all need to be proud of that story because it makes us stronger."

Taking action on Hartzell's experience

• Find a supportive member of senior management who can advocate for programs to mentor women in your organization.

• Identify the ROIs to demonstrate the benefits to the organization of programs designed to move women forward.

• Share your own story of rising up the corporate ladder to demonstrate the variety of ways women succeed.

Although the United States ranked first in women's educational attainment on the World Economic Forum's 2017 Global Gender Gap Index of 144 countries, it ranked 19th in women's economic participation and opportunity, and 96th in women's political empowerment.

World Economic Forum: The Global Gender Gap Report, 2018.

Evelyn Isaia
Cooking Up a Business Path for Women Immigrants

Evelyn Isaia's successful career in wealth management was so powerfully impacted by mentors that she felt an overwhelming obligation to pay it forward by developing the skills of women immigrants and refugees. So Isaia took early retirement and founded Ratatouille and Company, a Connecticut-based sophisticated catering company with a social purpose. Instead of advising the 1%-ers, she now employs, trains and mentors women from Syria, Haiti, Honduras, Guatemala, Colombia and El Salvador and will consider training any woman facing challenges, immigrant or not.

Isaia's goal is to provide these women with the skills they need to become successful in the culinary arts. It's working. One of Ratatouille's trainees has done so well, she has become garde manger (pantry chef) at one of Jean-Georges' restaurants.

Beyond culinary training, Isaia also provides a general support system that encourages personal growth, self-empowerment and self-advocacy. This includes guidance for getting fair wages and proper work hours; navigating temporary assistance programs; introductions to agencies such as the Small Business Administration, SCORE, and Women's

Business Development Council; and understanding their rights in the U.S. as opposed to their country of origin.

Isaia effected change by:

• Seeking out immigrant and refugee women with a desire to succeed in the culinary arts and giving them the training and opportunities to do it.

• Combining culinary technical training and hands-on experience with advice and resources for navigating life in the U.S.

• Mentoring these women to find their voice and advocate for themselves at work, at home and in the community.

* * *

In Isaia's own words

"I enjoy cooking, table setting and entertaining. So how could I put this all together and help women? I did a lot of searching, but it wasn't until a friend who is a restaurant owner and operator in New York City suggested we do a couple of catering events that it all started to come together. With her in the kitchen and me on the organizational and sales side, we were a great team. We thought Ratatouille was a cool name, so that's what we called it.

"Next we needed to have a workforce, so we have partnered with the International Rescue Committee (IRC) in New York City, Building One Community in Stamford, and the Connecticut Institute for Refugees and Immigrants in Bridgeport. We work with them to hire women who have an interest in the culinary arts, and we train them. I would say 98 percent of our workforce comes from these sources and, lately, also from Emma's Torch, another program in Brooklyn.

"I am especially proud of one of our mentees, Tatiana, who came to us through the culinary program at Building One Community in Stamford. She started as a server but was always interested in everything and wanted to learn more. So we started training her up because she really had a lot of talent and was a wonderful team member with great attitude. One of the members of our advisory board is Chef Ron Gallo at The Inn at Pound Ridge, one of Jean-Georges' restaurants. He arranged for Tatiana to interview with them and she started in the garde manger. Jean-Georges has also taken a second person from our program. It is the culmination of a dream, and we are only two years old!

"One of the unintended positive outcomes is every once in a while basing menus on our trainees' own cuisine culture. For example, when we catered a meal for the premiere of Alexandra Shiva's documentary, 'This Is Home: A Refugee Story,' we drew on some of the trainees' knowledge to create an authentic Syrian meal."

Taking action on Isaia's experience

• All things being equal, when you need a vendor or a service, have a bias for hiring businesses like Ratatouille that provide a path for women to advance.

• Offer yourself as a mentor or advisor to organizations that are working with female immigrant or refugee populations and preparing them for job searches.

• Start a business with a social mission, where your workforce is pulled from at-risk populations.

Women represent only 23 percent of the mayors of the 100 largest American cities.

Theresa Roden
Transforming Young Girls into Mentors and Leaders

Theresa Roden had never been athletic in school and grew up with a less-than-positive self-image. At age 35, with the support of a group of women friends/mentors, she completed what would be her first of many triathlons. Training for and completing the triathlon transformed her belief in herself and her abilities. With an 11-year-old daughter experiencing the same feelings of inadequacy and low self-esteem, Roden knew that if her daughter could learn at 11 what Roden had just learned at 35, her future would be dramatically better. And so i-tri (Inspirational Triathlon Racing International) was born.

I-tri fosters self-respect, empowerment, positive body image and healthy lifestyle choices for adolescent girls through the vehicle of training for triathlons. Ten years, 10 schools and hundreds of girls later, this grassroots organization is poised to begin a national expansion.

The program started as a pilot at Roden's daughter's school. They selected 10 girls who were not in any athletic program and prepared them for a youth triathlon, providing them with the training, mentoring and emotional support necessary to complete the event. Following the pilot season, those first 10 girls wanted to do it again the following year, each finding a new girl to mentor. To date, 700 girls have completed the program.

Roden effected change by:

• Giving young girls the role models and the formula to transform low self-esteem and body image into self-confidence and the ability to lead.

• Setting herself as a role model of how you can change your outlook by challenging yourself mentally and physically.

• Expanding the i-tri platform to include mentoring by professional women in business and exposure to life skills and STEM careers.

• Receiving mentorship from the highly successful women on i-tri's board as she herself transforms into a more formalized executive position within the growing organization.

* * *

In Roden's own words

"The journey of i-tri starts with my own journey. I was never an athletic kid; I always had low self-esteem and never felt proud of myself for anything I did. When I was in my mid-30s, I spent the summer on Block Island, off Rhode Island. One day I saw these crazy people running down the beach with numbers written in Sharpie on their arms, jumping over sandcastles. Everyone on the beach was cheering them on. I turned to a friend and asked, 'What are they doing?' 'The Block Island Triathlon,' he said. 'What's a triathlon?' I asked, and he explained it to me. That was my light-bulb moment. I said, 'You know what, I'm going to do this,' which was so outrageous even to contemplate, but I just knew it was right. I told a few of my girlfriends—we were all young moms at the time—and they said, 'That's a great idea. Why don't we all train together?'

"They were all pretty athletic women to begin with, and then there was me. But what happened was we all supported one another and we learned how to train as we went along. I also was going through an internal transition during this external transition, so I was changing the way I thought about myself. I knew that if I kept up the old internal dialogue of, 'I can't do this. I'm too fat. I'm too slow. I'm all of these things,' there was no way I was ever going to reach this goal. For the first time in my life, I had to be supportive, kind and encouraging to myself. That changed everything for me. I learned about affirmations and how powerful they are: 'I am strong, I am fast, I'm doing better today than I did yesterday, I will do it.'

"I also learned about visualization and seeing myself achieve my goal, living as if it had already happened. That is what got me to that finish line. And as great as the finish line moment was, and it was great, I realized that it was the journey from the day I had the idea until crossing the finish line, with the support from my friends and family, that changed my outlook.

"The real inspiration for i-tri was my daughter. She was 11 years old, and I was seeing in her a lot of the same things I had experienced. She wasn't going to be a team-sport girl. I knew the importance of that in a child's life, and I thought to myself, 'If I had learned what I know now at her age, what a difference it would have made.' What if we took a group of girls who don't consider themselves to be athletes, who may be struggling with self-esteem and self-confidence issues, and give them all the love and the support and the training and the equipment, everything they needed to do this really big goal?

"So I pitched the idea at my daughter's school and it was just miraculous because the school agreed to a pilot program. We started with 10 girls that first year, and it was one miracle after another making it all happen. They had an incredibly transformative experience. Eight of the girls who finished the race came back the second year and said, 'We love this so much that we want to do it again. We want to get more girls who can benefit to be a part of this.' They helped to create what i-tri is today: a regional program in 10 schools with 700 self-confident mentor graduates and a plan to take it to the national level. Our vision is that every single girl, anywhere in the world, who can benefit from i-tri, should have the opportunity to experience this transformational program.

"Four years ago, we began a 'Mentoring Day' and invited 60 professional women from different career fields and backgrounds to spend a day with the girls. This year, more than 160 girls participated in small-group mentoring sessions, as well as a whole-group networking session. The 11-year-old girls went way out of their comfort zones to approach judges, CEOs and business owners, looking them in the eye and introducing themselves as they shook hands and distributed their own business cards.

"The success of the Mentoring Day events and the desire of the mentors to become more involved, led to the creation of Mentor Circle Groups. Bringing together high-school-aged alumni with the committed mentors, the program includes learning table manners and basics of cooking, an architectural tour and a trip to a university neurobiology science lab. We are expanding in 2019 to accommodate more girls and mentors.

"We are now growing i-tri from a local grassroots organization into a regional and, soon, national, organization. And our staff also needs mentoring to do it all. Anne Starobin, who specializes in executive leadership development, and Linda Frankenbach, former CEO of fitsmi, are personally mentoring me in my new role as Executive Director and spokesperson. Adeline Neubert, a finance professional and business coach, has been mentoring Cindy Morris as she takes on the role of COO."

Taking action on Roden's experience

• Identify a young girl who you could train to enter an athletic competition, and along the way build her self-esteem and confidence.

• Challenge yourself to train with women friends to reach a physical goal or enter a competition, mentoring each other along the way.

• Offer yourself to a program or high school as a speaker or role model to show girls what they can become.

Bpeace has been proudly advancing women forward since 2002. More than 50 percent of the 250 businesses strengthened by Bpeace Skillanthropists are run by women.

Become a Skillanthropist

Bpeace (the Business Council for Peace) is the international nonprofit coalition of courageous, committed, optimistic business leaders. We believe that the best hope for long-term peace in historically violent communities is more jobs and the economic empowerment of women. We currently advise business owners in El Salvador, Guatemala and Lebanon.

When women work, violence in a region lessens.

When women lead, historically violent communities stabilize.

And when women business leaders have support, communities accelerate toward peace and prosperity.

Bpeace is committed to a world where women business leaders in historically violent communities have the tools and support to grow, create good jobs and succeed.

More jobs mean less violence®

The Bpeace model unites high-quality business consulting by volunteers ("Skillanthropists") with proven and promising local job creators ("Fast Runners") to help these business owners break through the barriers to growth and job creation.

Bpeace offers 5-star on-the-ground and remote volunteer opportunities for Skillanthropists to advise international business owners and job creators. For those on both sides of this equation, the impact of the work they do together is measurable.

Could your business skills and experience accelerate peace and prosperity in a community that needs both?

Learn more at *bpeace.org, greatnonprofits.org,*
or email us at *womenforward@bpeace.org.*

Made in the USA
Middletown, DE
26 July 2019